A
STONE
DIARY

A STONE DIARY

Pat Lowther

Toronto
Oxford University Press
1977

Some of these poems were first published in *Antigonish Review,
Blackfish, The Canadian Forum, Event, The Fiddlehead, For Neruda/
For Chile, Inscape (Ottawa), Inscape (U.S.), Lakehead University
Review, Mainline, Mountain Moving Day, Quarry, Skookum Wawa,
University of Windsor Review, West Coast Review, Woman's Eye.*

Publication of this book was assisted by the Canada Council.
© Oxford University Press (Canada) 1977
ISBN 19-5402618
1 2 3 4 — 10 9 8 7
Printed in Canada by John Deyell Company

CONTENTS

CONTENTS

3

1

A STONE DIARY

At the beginning I noticed
the huge stones on my path
I knew instinctively
why they were there
breathing as naturally
as animals
I moved them to ritual patterns
I abraded my hands
and made blood prints

Last week I became
aware of details
cubes of fool's gold
green and blue copper
crystal formations
fossils   shell casts
iron roses   candied gems

I thought of
the Empress Josephine,
the Burning of Troy
between her breasts,
of Ivan the Terrible lecturing
on the virtues of rubies.
They were dilettantes.

By the turn of the week
I was madly in love
with stone. Do you know
how beautiful it is
to embrace stone
to curve all your body
against its surfaces?

Yesterday I began
seeing you as
desirable as a stone
I imagined you coming
onto the path with me
even your mouth
a carved stone

Today for the first time
I noticed how coarse
my skin has grown
but the stones shine
with their own light,
they grow smoother
and smoother

RUMOURS OF WAR

In my very early years
I must have heard
ominous news broadcasts
on the radio;
they must have mentioned
the Black Forest

for I dreamed a black forest
moving across a map,
I and my rag doll
caught on the coast edge
of the country
I was too young
even to name

Austria Poland Hungary
would have meant nothing
to me
but the Black Forest
came right up our ravine
down over the mountains

and Raggedy Ann
and I woke screaming
out of the clutch of
evil trees

EARLY WINTERS

Under the burned-off mountain
winds died   the forest rangers
packed their sleeping bags
and left for town
trees cracked their knuckles
windows began telling stories

And the child dreamed meteors
spiralling like snowflakes
into the trees

Herbs in the garden died
bees slept in their cells
a late bear tumbled the garbage cans
the creek broke ice
and rushed endlessly past the house

And the child dreamed blue water
green water
and the death of water

Deer on the winter road
wore jewels in their antlers
the spines of the burnt mountain
sifted the snow
like a giant comb

And the child dreamed passionate singers
gathering mountains before them
irresistible as the wind

The sky stayed white all night
the valley rocked
with the speed of the creek
breathing a sound like a shell

And the child dreamed all
trees   mountains
the unknown singers
luminous and falling
as softly as the snow

PRIVATE OWNERSHIP

The peacocks scream
on Curlew Island
owned by a Texas Millionaire
guarded by Fierce Dogs
and Peacocks
(don't beach a boat there
you'll be savaged by mastiffs,
lashed by the clacking
tails of peacocks)
Peacocks are more alert
than dogs, but stupid:
gulls set them off
or mocking crows
or boys across the channel
on the public beach.
Soon there's a wild concert
Gulls Crows Boys and Peacocks
screaming again and again
till the Dogs catch
the hysteria, bark insanely.
Out comes the Millionaire,
paunch wobbling or
bony fist shuddering
(of course I've never seen him,
he's probably a Thing of Beauty
his physique as carefully guarded
as Curlew Island)
Nobody's ever seen him
but we hear his voice:
Shuddup, you gawdam dogs !
Shuddup !

INHERITANCE

Annie McCain bequeathed to me
her lace:
tatting   crocheting
yards and yards of
ecru and cream and white
spiderweb pattern   pineapple
doilies and tablecloth edging

She must have imagined me
in the citrus smell
of furniture polish
gleaming walnut and oak
pouring tea from a silver pot

She should have known even then
I'd be something else
useless at owning things
up to my head in books

But she gave me lace.
I'd rather have had
her old corsets
that I fastened for her
with mighty heaves,
or her brass bed
where I slept in the warm
dent she made
early mornings
I'd rather have her rockingchair
I coveted half my life

Twenty-five years in tissue
wraps, Annie McCain's lace
runs through my all-thumbs
like something I can't
even regret.
It's turning slowly amber
like her beautiful hair
that never went gray
in a long life of making

NIGHTMARE

Edgar Allen Poe &
Disney combined
couldn't have done it
better: the tall black house
the dungeon
the secret book

Later, the pale determined
men with dogs.
I try to cry out:
I'm harmless !
but the words can't
get through my fangs.

CHACABUCO, THE PIT

(Information filtered out of Chile: political
prisoners formerly held in the stadium at Santiago
have been transported to a Nazi-type concentration
camp set up in a disused nitrates mine somewhere
on the Atacama desert.)

EVERYTHING SHOULD BE DONE
QUIETLY AND EFFECTIVELY TO INSURE
THAT ALLENDE DOES NOT LAST THE NEXT
CRUCIAL SIX MONTHS.
— from 18-point plan submitted by International
Telegraph and Telephone Co. to the White House, USA.

CONTACT TRUSTWORTHY SOURCES
WITHIN THE CHILEAN ARMED FORCES.
— from Point 7, above.

*I shall speak to the Lord of Heaven
where he sits asleep.*
— from an ancient Mayan prayer.

Atacama desert:
by day the sun lets down
his weight   everyone wears
a halo   everything quivers
sharp-sided dust refracts
blurred glitter between
creased squinting eyelids;
by night the land is naked
to the farthest reaches
between galaxies
that vacuum sucks
heat: the land is
cold to the utter bone.

Carefully now (place
records on a turntable)
remember those 1940s movies
where virgins were sacrifices
to volcanoes: here is
that same
        ceremonial
            suspenseful
                approach:
we are approaching
            Chacabuco
                the pit.

Notice first the magnificent sunset,
the stars, the clouds of Magellan.
Note that here as in all human places
prayer has been uttered.

Watch until morning
burns the sky white.
Wooden shacks persevere
in the dry air,
their corners banked with dust;
a grid of streets prints
an ominous white shadow
on your eyelids;
it leads
to the pit.

A huge, gouged cavity
flickering like a bad film,
the whole scene twitching
on and off
in and out of existence:
is God blinking? are you
shuttering your eyes, tourista?

I shall speak to the lord of heaven
where he sits asleep

there are men in that pit
imagine that they are chained
(they may be)

starving (they are)
watched over by jailers
with faces blank
as a leached brain

Working, that sallow bitter rock
ground to glass
powder enters their lungs
nostrils eyes pores
Sleeping, they dream of eating
rock, sucking juice from it
pissing nitrate dust

Moments of darkness film
their eyes, they stumble
in negative light
and the blows of whips

Do they remember
who they are? patriots
        believers
                builders

collective dreamers who woke
to find all their good wishes
happening faster
than they could move,
the people outreaching the planners
factory workers running
the factories
children wearing moustaches
of milk

Forgetting to keep guns beside their pillows
forgetting to bribe generals
breathing long breaths of peace
organizing anti-Fascist song festivals
instead of militia
seeing the people stand at last
upright in mellow light like a sound harvest
they forgot lifetimes of exile
years of held breath and stealth
seeing so many strong
they forgot the strength of I.T.&T.
United Fruit Co.
                Anaconda

who do not easily give up
what they have taken.

✳

Some one decides
who shall eat
who shall not eat
who shall be beaten
and on which
parts of his body

Some one decides
who shall be starved
who shall be fed
enough to sustain
another day's torture

A man decides.
That man does not breathe dust:
he is dust.

Choirs of young boys
exquisitely trained
sing hymns in cathedrals;
jellyfish swim in the ocean
like bubbles of
purity made tangible;
whole cities lie open
to the stars;
women bake bread;
fruit trees unfold their blossoms
petal by petal;
we are continually born

but these, captive, stumble
in gross heat
in stupor of pain:
they are the fingers sliced off
when the wood was cut,
the abortions born living;
they are the mangled
parts of our bodies
screaming to be
reunited.

'If I forget thee, O Zion

Let statesmen's tongues lock
between their jaws,
let businessmen's cheque hands
be paralyzed,
let musicians stop building
towers of sound,
let commerce fall
in convulsions:
we have deserved this.

Staircases ascending
through caverns
clefts in the root sockets
of mountains, opening
onto ocean's foot:
we have all been there,
that journey, its
hardships its surprises
stay in our cells
our footprints in clay
splayed: we were burdened.

Remember breathing on fire
a cautious husbandry
then suddenly sparks
bursting upward
like dolphins leaping
in the sunlight path
of the first boat
we had song
       mathematics
           magic

Even for torturers we have done this
journey, broken
ourselves like crumbs,
pumped children into wombs,
heaved them out,
laid stone on stone;

we forgive each other
our absurdities,
casually accept splendour;
we forgive even death

but these places
of death slowly inflicted
we can't forgive, but writhe
coiling in on ourselves
to try to forget, to deny:
*we have travelled so far
and these are still with us?*

Even now in our cities
churches   universities
pleasant lawns   we are
scrabbling with broken nails
against rock, we are
dying of flies and disease.
Until that pus is drained
we are not healed.

'And the dead shall be raised incorruptible'

When their names are called
will you answer,
will I?

for bread on the table
for salt in the bread
for bees in the cups
of flowers
will you answer to their names?

For I tell you the earth
itself is a mystery
which we penetrate constantly
and our people a holy mystery
beyond refusal

And the horrors of the mind
are the horrors of
what we allow to be done
and the grace of the soul
is what we determine shall be
made truly among us. Amen.

LEONARD GEORGE
AND, LATER, A ROCK BAND

Do you know you can
talk to trees
do you know
stones are alive
do you know birds
fish   water   a song
for every position of the sun

In lieu of guns or tears
he raises these
against the bricked eyes
of the speculators

His memory rooted
in specific magic
of land alive
When the trees go
he won't be here

To speak from the cramped edges
against their assumption
of his death
he says first his true name
and the names of his father
and grandfather

With those syllables
unique   unshared

he brings it altogether
against them
a man whole
in the broken world

2

Netting the random air
with their drums,
cymbals, demanding electrons,
for them sooner
than for us it comes together,
a geodesic web of sound
in which their freedom's
their contained dimension.

Now with their easy will,
with the power
of having it whole,
they move it outward
to contain us.
We are altogether
touching in the warm electric
balloon, dependent
on a cord, a plug.

NOTES FROM FURRY CREEK

1

The water reflecting cedars
all the way up
deep sonorous green—
nothing prepares you
for the ruler-straight
log fallen across
and the perfect
water fall it makes
and the pool behind it
novocaine-cold
and the huckleberries
hanging
like fat red lanterns

2

The dam, built
by coolies, has outlived
its time; its wall
stained sallow
as ancient skin
dries in the sun

The spillway still
splashes bright spray
on the lion
shapes of rock
far down below

The dam foot
is a pit
for the royal animals
quiet and dangerous
in the stare
of sun and water

3

When the stones swallowed me
I could not surface
but squatted
in foaming water
all one curve
motionless,
glowing like agate.

I understood the secret
of a monkey-puzzle tree
by knowing its opposite:

the smooth and the smooth
and the smooth takes,
seduces your eyes
to smaller and smaller
ellipses;
reaching the centre
you become
stone, the perpetual
lavèd god.

THE EARTH SINGS MI-FA-MI

'. . . so we can gather even from this
that MIsery and FAmine reign on
our habitat.' — Johannes Kepler,
a footnote to *Harmonice Mundi.*

Outside the U.S. consulate
in freezing wind
the street theatre group
arranges space within
the crowd

The girl who represents
the Vietnamese people
wears a black body
stocking and a mask
I thought at first
patronizing
but as the mime unfolds
its over-human contours
and its broken eyes
immovable
become a perfect image
for us all

Those of us near
the players sing with them
softly shouldering aside
our inhibitions
Ho Ho Ho Chi Minh
hoping our soft noise
will spread outward
from the centre

But the wind screams
and the earth spinning
like notes uttered
like whipped wires
the earth sings Mi-Fa-Mi

January 1973

FACE

it's said a leader loses
something seen
in the flesh smaller
than his image on
the cool gray t.v.
choosing words
precisely as specified
pincers and screws;
seeing in the street's
light, his egg face
greased with anxiety,
tension of a present crowd
hostile, is more whole-
some: seeing a leader
sweat in the face
of the people.

COAST RANGE

Just north of town
the mountains start to talk
back-of-the-head buzz
of high stubbled meadows
minute flowers
moss gravel and clouds

They're not snobs, these mountains,
they don't speak Rosicrucian,
they sputter with
billygoat-bearded creeks
bumsliding down
to splat into the sea

they talk with the casual
tongues of water
rising in trees

They're so humble they'll let you
blast highways through them
baring their iron and granite
sunset-coloured bones
broken for miles

And nights when
clouds foam on a beach
of clear night sky,
those high slopes creak
in companionable sleep

*

Move through gray green
aurora of rain
to the bare fact:
The land is bare.

Even the curly opaque Pacific
forest, chilling you full awake
with wet branch-slaps,
is somehow bare
stainless as sunlight:

The land is what's left
after the failure
of every kind of metaphor.

The plainness of first things
trees
gravel
rocks
naive root atom
of philosophy's first molecule

The mountains reject nothing
but can crack
open your mind
just by being intractably there

Atom: that which can not
be reduced

You can gut them
blast them
to slag
the shapes they've made in the sky
cannot be reduced

DARK

I tell you the darkness comes down
like arrows and hunger
I tie knots in my hair
to remember other empires
The world falls through my forehead
resistlessly as rain

I must tell you I can not
always move with decorum
The darkness comes down like meteors
petals of hot black
I escape burning only because
I am the darkness

2

SONG

If I take you to my island
you'll have to remember
to speak quietly
you'll have to remember
sound carries over water
You must come by night
we'll walk through the dark
orchards to the sea
and gather crystal jellyfish
from the black water
we'll lie on the sand
and feel the galaxy
on our cheeks and foreheads
you'll have to remember
to wear warm clothing
follow where I go
and speak very softly
if I take you

ANEMONES

Under the wharf at Saturna
the sea anemones
open their velvet bodies

chalk black
          and apricot
                    and lemon-white

they grow as huge
and glimmering
          as flesh chandeliers

under the warped
and salt-stained wharf
    letting down
        their translucent mouths
                          of arms

even the black ones
have an aura
like an afterimage of light

Under our feet
    the gorgeous animals
        are feeding
                    in the sky

OCTOPUS

The octopus is beautifully
functional as an umbrella;
at rest a bag of rucked skin
sags like an empty scrotum
his jelled eyes sad and bored

but taking flight: look
how lovely purposeful
in every part:
the jet vent smooth
as modern plumbing
the webbed pinwheel of tentacles
moving in perfect accord
like a machine dreamed
by Leonardo

CRANEFLIES IN THEIR SEASON

Struggling in the grass
or splayed against walls and fences,
they seem always somehow askew.
Even their flights in air
appear precarious
and all their moves seem
to be accidents.

Dead, they form windrows
of bent wires,
broken delicate parts
of some unexplained machine.
And the wind sweeps them
like evidence of an accident
out of sight.

HERMIT CRABS

In a pool maybe the size
of a man's forearm
there are hundreds of them,
little curled amber
snail shells scuttling sideways
like no snails.
You can just see
their brindle legs
fine as the teeth of a fine-tooth
tortoiseshell comb.
Five of them might
cover my fingernail,
but poke one
and he'll put out pincers
thin as bronze wire
and dare you
to do it again.

SLUGS

Yellow gray
          boneless things
    like live phlegm
heaving themselves
gracelessly
across sidewalks

44

laboured
as though the earth
were not their element
oozing their viscid mess
    for godsake don't
                step
                    there
ugh ugh
horrible pulp

: two of them:
the slime from their bodies
makes a crystal rope
            suspending
them   in air
        under
    the apple tree

    they are twined
            together
in a perfect spiral
    flowing
                around
    eath other
            spinning
    gently
            with their motions
Imagine
        making love like that

SUSPENDED

When you choose silence
I shall be like
the last rain
         drop
on a tree branch
  waiting to fall

Imagine that I contain
    branch   tree
  butterflies   snakes
the entire forest
   a sun
hardly a pin-prick's size
   but bright enough
   to spear your eye

WRESTLING

Lover I must
approach you as Jacob
to his angel,
rough with that need.
Yes I will
pin you down,
force answers from you;
I will make sense
of you, place you
like a planet
or constellation
in my known zodiac:
First fall.

BIRTHDAYS

1

You say you were born
a time and place
foreign to me;
i can't imagine
where you come from
though you wear your past
like articulated flesh,
a body learned
and exercised

how have you disguised
your battles
that i see
you without scars,
assume them only
as one assumes
the tough mechanics
of heart and bowels

i know there
must have been darkness
fish thrashing in blood
that stinging slash
where light breaks
: metamorphoses

2

just as you breaking
into, displace me,
thrust me under
my own past, i have
to go through
it all again;
nothing will come out
any differently,
but i will

: one of those
places where the surface
breaks like water
clashes and chops
of light, far under
everything is shifted
everything moves

3

all nerves ending
in air make the shape
of a birthday, the shape
set out: 'Go'
some other stranger says

and walking flying
you move toward
more birthdays
than anyone
expects or celebrates

GREETINGS FROM THE INCREDIBLE SHRINKING WOMAN

it's not that
i'm getting smaller
(i thought so at first)
but that the continent's
expanding, stretching
like silly putty
or like a movie
seen in a dream

landmarks, even back fences,
recede; where i am
is always empty

i used to see myself
at the land's edge
waiting maybe to be
flicked off,
to thrash like a fish
in the saltchuck

now it's miles from
my house even
to the Fraser River
which is immense,
swollen like throat-veins

and the landscape continues
to pull out
while i do nothing

just by standing
here, i'm dwindling
to a dot.
(actually it's that
i'm finally learning
perspective)

ANNIVERSARY LETTER TO PABLO

That first time
on the moongravel
they jumped like clumsy fawns.
They were drunk in love
with their own history;
Satori flash lighted
their indelible footprints.

But you warmed the moon
in a loving cup,
in the thawing
water of your eyes,
you the man who moves
under the hill,
the man who kisses stone.

Custodians of footsteps
and magnets,
you take mineral glitter
in the cup
of your hand,
it becomes veins.
You own also the moon
now where they touched.

LETTER TO PABLO 2

Even on this spatter
of islands
would you find finger bones
washed up on beaches,
heelprints round as embraces
in the salt rock?

You would know where
the clamshell middens are;
you would be plunged
so wholly in that feast
the cooking fire would burn
still in the deep bowl
of your belly.

Even here between the edges
of the elements
you would be crouched
transmuting delicate fossils
out of foam.

LETTER TO PABLO 3

Honouring your dead
with fat of meat
with well-crusted bread
with honey and garlic,
old man licking oil
off your thumbs and belching,
you are more lustrous
than flowers.
Carnations, poppies,
their spice and bravura
fall in a dusting
of petals shaken;
you move past the image
to honour the belly
the hands   the jaws and teeth,
the incense of cooking
the sacrament of bread.

LETTER TO PABLO 4

It isn't easy
to keep moving thru
the perpetual motion
of surfaces,
the web of skin and glances

Are you there
always at the centre
like Buddha contemplating
the heart
of the plural self?
: constant joy
like a fountain
still even in motion

All my life I wanted
that holy water
to well like stigmata
in my palms.
the skin the skin
is so subtle
and so hard to evade

LAST LETTER TO PABLO

Under the hills and veins water
comes out like stars;
your spirit
fleshy palpable
mines in the earth
dung and debris of generations;
curled shells
rags of leaves
impress your palms

I imagine you
a plateau city
spangled with frost,
a blue electric wind
before nightfall
that touches and takes
the breath away

How many making love
in the narrow darkness
between labours
how many bodies laid
stone upon stone
generations of fire and dirt
before you broke from us
a whole branch flowering

Cancer the newscast said,
and coma,   but
what of the sea
also full of bones
and miracles
they said was your
last prison?
What of your starward-riding
cities creaking again
with steel?   How long
is death?

We are weary of atrocities;
the manure of blood
you said grows
something so frightful
only you could look:
you smoothing wounds
we shudder from —
bloody leather
face forming in mud

Always earth was
your substance:
grain, ores and bones
elements folded in power
humans patient as time
and weather;
now you too lie with skeletons
heaped about you;
our small crooked hands
touch you for comfort

From the deep hollows
water comes out like stars;
you are changing, Pablo,
becoming an element
a closed throat of quartz
a calyx
imperishable in earth

As our species bears
the minute electric
sting, possibility,
our planet carries Neruda
bloodstone
dark jewel of history
the planet carries you
a seed patient as time.

3

I.D.

i want to say
tell me
who you are,
and you give me
a clear answer,
who you are

then i think of
the question reversed
like a knife
bladed toward me
tell me
who you are

:i'm a blunder
a mouth, crying
a figure running
with hands upright
at right angles
to the arms

and i think after
all i won't
ask you
who you are

SPITBALL

His hands flicker
brown on the white
costume, the green arena;
a shuttling dance,
all stations touched
Earth, thighs,
heart, the head
covering, the mouth
also moves, chewing
herbs and invocations.
The hands weave wind,
the watchers' tension,
prayers, sweat
from the forehead,
and unseen in the swift
dazzle of motion
the magic spittle
points the ball.

LEVITATION

It's only belief
sets us up in contradiction
to the universe;
even just standing still
we're going
against the grain

Last night the student
talking about writing:
his body began to curve
to cave over me
I raised my hands
for his weight
I thought maybe we could
crumple together
painlessly

——suddenly straightened
and fell full length
away from me
striking the back of his head
like wood breaking and I standing there
had not saved
that blow

People who knew how
counted pulse beats,
massaged, but not until
he came back to his eyes
could he lift off
the flat surface

It's only thinking we can
lets us defy the law
of gravity;
even standing
talking about writing
is a kind of
Indian rope trick

100

Yes he is full now
like an articulated shell,
fragile, enclosing liquid.
The slightest thing
brims his eyes:
any emotion
or a minute lapse
of memory, self-doubt;
his lips tremble
like black moths' wings,
his eyes blue
as watered milk startle
through lenses of tears.
He cannot speak
to you, to anyone,
without these tears
surprising him.
His hand inky with veins
falters toward your wrist,
your arm: touch
anchors him here, upright.
There is an urgent message
fluttering
like his pulse,
a prayer, a summation.
Always, from breath to breath,
he is saying goodbye.

TO A WOMAN WHO DIED OF 34 STAB WOUNDS

I can see it as though I'd been there,
you pouring beer and talking,
your heavy scarlet smile
held out like a credit card.
Glances would cross behind your back
(you'd have been quite spectacular
then, in the way a reconstruction
of the San Francisco Opera House
would be spectacular)
They wouldn't know
that milky velvet you affected
was your true face.

In your prime you'd seduce anyone,
woman or man, considering that
the friendly thing to do.
Your murderer couldn't believe
so much pride could survive
in flesh gone soft.
At the end, coiling, striking,
his rage was for himself,
for his fine body failing
to humble your sagging sixty.

REFLECTING SUNGLASSES

Circles of sky
and storefronts in my face—
look through me:
lattice of moving air
chrome   sunburst   faces—
I'm a see-through woman
proof enough of
the proposition that we're all
mostly
empty space.
I swing along carrying
tunnels of vision
through the imaginary fabric
of my brain.
Lean closer and you'll see
you looking out
from me.

CITY SLIDE / 1

The fish pushes the
fine net into
one of the large
holes of the coarse net

We arrange spaces
within
spaces
sixes and sevens
sticks and stones
inside us
the large holes
and the fine holes
are silted
with data

Arranging my rectangular
soapbox
between a mens
and a stone lion
thereby eclipsing the sun
for anything shorter than me,
I declaim:
My Fellow Conspirators

Citizens, file your teeth
the big ones
and the small ones.
he's only a string man
destroy him
with terrible smiles

CITY SLIDE / 2

For Hugh Jordan

You are strolling thru downtown
with spicy pinks
braided into your moustache.
Your girl being surfeited with answers,
her expression becomes almost severe.
Your little son is bare naked.

Having broken down all the official buildings
by standing against them doing isometrics,
you are unconcerned that the sky
could want to eat you.
You might even toss a few peanuts
into its lewdly stretching jaws.

CITY SLIDE / 3

Wilfred Barrett regards the street
as his apartment
and statues
as very tall acquaintances.
From a gum wrapper's viewpoint
the world's an intimate:
he can't understand
about jaywalking.

Wilfred Barrett's the lost
dollar bill
of a bad conscience.
He is the face that remains
beautiful
when everything else has gone bad,
that keeps rising out
of your crotch and bosom,
warm places where it clings
like an unwanted pet.
Wilfred Barrett tempts me
to sentimentality,
tempts me to imagine myself
giving smiles
as if they were jewels and bread.

Wilfred Barrett's a great
respecter of symbols,
reacting to uniforms
as a dog to fleas.
Confident of pavement,
he accepts a cigarette
or a Vag B bust
with equal poise.

Philosophy breaks in him
like bubbles
struggling up through mash.
Head up against
the sooty sun,
he turns your patronage
into a wound, a memory
of guilty love.

CITY SLIDE / 5

A vine at my window
scratches only gently

the city breathes like
a warm herbivorous mammal

violence among the cells
only a vague pain
below consciousness

the animal sleeps
waiting unknowingly

for a virus
from another climate
to test its viability

CITY SLIDE / 6

Love is an intersection
where I have chosen
unwittingly to die

Next year the blue lights
will still be here
lighting up columns of rain

I'll be in a room
in this same city
with my sick headache
reflecting on accidents
of all kinds

CITY SLIDE / 7

There is another level
I almost remember:
streets unfold
like the gestures of fountains
graceful as water's
necessities
down where the lighted towers
spiral to vegetable
roots unthreatening
there are cliffs in the city
you will not fall.
but climbing
you will suddenly again
put down your foot *here.*
As you said
(and how could you know
 already the grey
 hardening in your limbs)
––Christ O Christ, no one lives long.

IT HAPPENS EVERY DAY

children crawl into
dumped refrigerators;
trappers alone on snowfields
step in their own snares;
women court dangerous men
who will beat them to death.

on the other hand
it isn't the landlord
who dies when a tenement burns;
the housewife who puts up
botulism in jars
takes her whole family with her;
hunters who wear red jackets
still get shot.

KITCHEN MURDER

Everything here's a weapon:
i pick up a meat fork,
imagine
plunging it in,
a heavy male
thrust

in two hands
i heft a stone-
ware plate, heavy
enough?

rummage the cupboards:
red pepper, rape-
seed oil, Drano

i'll wire myself
into a circuit:
the automatic perc,
the dishwater, the
socket above the sink

i'll smile an electric
eel smile:
whoever touches
me is dead.

INTERSECTION

At Fraser & Marine, slapped
by the wind from
passing traffic

light standards, trolleys
everything has edges
too real to touch

taxis unload at the hotel
the Gulf station fills them up

the lego apartment block
is sharp as salt

And the sunset is tea rose
colour strained, clarified
between navy-blue clouds,
the moon in its first
immaculate crescent

it's an axis
    double intersection
        transparencies

the thumb end
where you press
and the whole universe twirls out
a long seamless skin
a rill of piano music

the calla lily is seamless
yet divided

that cream skin wall
deceives the eye
following round and around
like fingers on ivory

refractions hook under
the eyelashes
you imagine that you can see
honeycombs
    jewels
     individual cells

texture reveals nothing;

to touch is to bruise

diesel trucks negotiate
left turns,
their long trailers creaking

headlights spurt
at the green signals

it was just here
at this bus stop
I lost my glove
my forty-cent transfer
my book
of unwritten profundities

I tell you they fell upward !
I saw them
      glinting
          catching light
from the thin, solid moon

The Blue Boy Motor Hotel
advertises:
try our comfortably
refurbished rooms
with color TV

the clouds are ink-blue
in the west

mercury lights lie along
the streets' contours
like strings of blue rhinestones

the bus stop bench
is painted blue, it
advertises Sunbeam bread

Don't touch the bench
it could burn you
or crystallize
your molecules with cold

keep your eyes on the sidewalk,
not paved here,
the puddles from recent rain

the Gulf station
could swallow you like a prairie

you could walk into
that phone booth
and step out between the planets

HOTLINE TO THE GULF

1

A hot wire
into the immense
turquoise
chasm of silence

this slenderest serpent
electrode fanged
excruciatingly
delicately
into my jugular
snaking under my ear
down to the heart's
chambers

it brings me new
perceptions: the world
is not a sphere,
it's a doughnut,
there's a huge
hole at the centre

away down there
are clouds,
a static of voices
remote as angels

2

Write to me, darling
from the other world.
send me olives.

3

There was this woman
on the radio:
all you had to do
was phone CJOR
and she'd give you
the inside dope
on your loved ones
Passed Beyond.

Turning the dial,
what I heard was
my sister's voice:
What can you tell me
about my little boy?

And I ripped the cord
from the wall,
beat my fists
on the kitchen
counter, crying
against that reaching
more terrible
even than death.

4

A list of things done
with hot wires:
    cauterizing small wounds
    burning off warts
    removing the eyes
    of caged songbirds
    shoving it up the penis
    of prisoners

5

Speak to me
for Gods sake.
There are worse things
than death
though you and I
are not likely
to experience
any of them

6

I could almost climb
that wire down
hand over hand
like a fine chain
dangling
into the cool
abyss

a faint odour
of absence,
windless air,
buzzing
of distant voices
I can't recognize

7

Or that imaginary
ribcage
which sheltered me like
a white picket fence
built with love
expanded,
rushed outward
out of sight:

I'm a red
thing beating
at the centre
of emptiness

only a hot vein
wires me
to the perimeter
straining
to hear syllables
in the hiss of blood

SUICIDES

Men on the lips
of high windows
women on bridges
or walking steadily
into water
—no. Think of height
water perhaps
but first air,
plumb trajectories
carving air
our gallant proxies
dropping from
high places
dropping like whole branches
of apples
dropping like meteors
dropping like an invasion
from outer space
worlds in collision
dropping like bombs
on Indo-China
dropping like spent
fireworks (matter
is what falls back
from the luminous high-
arching parabola
of energy: Bergson,

a paraphrase)
sizzling through the air
like jet trails
you can wish on
them as if they were
gifts of nature
the fatal acrobats
falling for
you and me

THE DIG

Even where traffic passes
the ancient world has exposed
a root, large and impervious,
humped like a dragon
among the city's conduits.
Look, they say,
who would have thought
the thing so tough,
so secretive?

The Diggers

The bone gloved in clay
shallow perhaps where arches
of feet go over;
they see it as finished
round like a jar;
a shard they see as whole.
Will our bones tell
what we died of?

The diggers
with very gentle fingers
lift up the bones of a woman;
tenderly they take off
her stockings of earth;
they have not such love
for the living
who are not finished
or predicted.

The Bones

The men we see always swift
moving, edged with a running light
like fire; their hands infinitely
potent, working in blood,
commanding the death of animals,
the life of the tribe.

The women we see finished
completed like fat jars,
like oil floating on water:
breasts   bellies   faces
all round and calm.

Their bones should thrash
in the diggers' baskets,
should scream against the light.

Their work bent them
and sex, that soft explosion
miraculous as rain
broke in them over and over,
their bodies thickened like tubers
broke and were remade
again and again crying out
in the heave of breaking
the terrible pleasure
again and again till
they fell away, at last
they became bone.

Even their hands
curved around implements,
pounding-stones, were worshipping
the cock that made them
round and hollow.

But before their falling away
was an anger,
a stone in the mouth.
They would say there is
a great fall like water,
a mask taking shape on air,
a sound coming nearer
like a heavy animal
breaking twigs.

And the flesh stamen
bursting inside them
splayed their bones
apart like spread legs.

Will our bones tell
sisters, what we died of?
how love broke us
in that helplessly desired
breaking, and men
and children ransacked our flesh,
cracked our innermost bones
to eat the morrow.

CATARACT

First everything turns to rainbows
edges of bronze and blue
doppler colour,
seen through a fine curtain
or the continual cast up
spray from a great fall.

Later the curtain thickens
white fog obscures shapes
hearing grows tense
for the rush and pressure
of blood like a great river
gathering volume
falling among caverns
in the listening skull

rushing toward the gorge
thunder and rub
to the precipice under the ear
to dive like Niagara
into the abyss
the hollow continent
the body

He is locked in
the white space
the mist   and the cataract
of blood he is forced
now to hear   and sways
like earth shaken
by its passage.

IN THE SILENCE BETWEEN

In the silence between the
notes of music
something is moving:
an animal
with the eyes of a man
multitudes
clothed in leaves

It is as if huge
migrations take place
between the steps
of music
like round
stones in water:
what flows between is
motion so constant
it seems still

Is it only the heart
beat
suspended
like a planet
in the hollow body

messages of blood
or the sensed arrival
of photons
from the outer
galaxies?

A journey that far
we begin also
advancing
between
progressions of music
the notes make
neuron
paths where we move
between earths
our heads full of leaves
our eyes like
the eyes of humans

DATE DUE